OUR LIVING WORLD: EARTH'S BIOMES

Oceans, Seas, and Reefs

Barbara A. Somervill

TRADITION BOOKS®, MAPLE PLAIN, MINNESOTA

A NEW TRADITION IN CHILDREN'S PUBLISHING™

ABOUT THE AUTHOR

Barbara A. Somervill is the author

of many books for children. She loves

learning and sees every writing

project as a chance to learn new

information or gain a new under-

standing. Ms. Somervill grew up in

New York State, but has also lived in

Toronto, Canada; Canberra, Australia;

California; and South Carolina. She

currently lives with her husband in

Simpsonville, South Carolina.

CONTENT ADVISER

Susan Woodward, Professor of

Geography, Radford University,

Radford, Virginia

In gratitude to George R. Peterson Sr. for introducing me to the beauty of creation
—George R. Peterson Jr., Publisher, Tradition Books®

Published in the United States of America by Tradition Books® and distributed to the school and library market by The Child's World®

[ACKNOWLEDGMENTS]
For Editorial Directions, Inc.: E. Russell Primm, Editorial Director; Dana Meachen Rau, Line Editor; Katie Marsico, Associate Editor; Judi Shiffer, Associate Editor and Library Media Specialist; Matthew Messbarger, Editorial Assistant; Susan Hindman, Copy Editor; Lucia Raatma, Proofreaders; Ann Grau Duvall, Peter Garnham, Deborah Grahame, Katie Marsico, Elizabeth K. Martin, and Kathy Stevenson, Fact Checkers; Tim Griffin/IndexServ, Indexer; Cian Loughlin O'Day, Photo Researcher; Linda S. Koutris, Photo Selector

For The Design Lab: Kathleen Petelinsek, design, art direction, and cartography; Kari Thornborough, page production

[PHOTOS]
Cover/frontispiece: Stock Photos/Corbis.
Interior: Animals Animals/Earth Scenes: 11 (Gerard Lacz), 28 (Bob Cranston), 52 (W. Gregory Brown), 61 (OSF/ D. Fleetham), 73 (Doug Wechsler), 90 (C. C. Lockwood); Yann Arthus-Bertrand/Corbis: 74, 81; Bettmann/Corbis: 4, 72, 86; Phillip Colla/Oceanlight.com: 46; Brandon D. Cole: 34, 71; Brandon D. Cole/Corbis: 64, 69; Corbis: 8 (David Ball), 9 (Paul A. Souders), 18 (Guy Motil), 23 (Lloyd Cliff), 35 (Alissa Crandall), 47 (Wolfgang Kaehler), 48 (Jeffrey L. Rotman), 49 (Stuart Westmorland), 50 (Robert Pickett), 55 (Lester V. Bergman), 62 (Ralph A. Clevenger), 67 (Amos Nachoum), 78 (Alan Schein Photography), 83 (Sean Sexton Collection), 85 (Joel W. Rogers), 88 (Natalie Fobes), 89 (Nik Wheeler), 91 (Tom Bean); Michael DeFreitas: 26; E. R. Degginger/Dembinsky Photo Associates: 24; Digital Vision: 14, 25, 32, 45, 80, 84; Stephen Frink: 42, 60; Getty Images/Brand X Pictures: 12, 19; François Gohier: 29; Jeff Jacobsen/François Gohier: 38; Breck P. Kent: 43; Jacques Langevin/Corbis Sygma: 56; NASA/GSFC: 6; NOAA/OAR/National Undersea Research Program/National Marine Fisheries Service/Woods Hole Lab: 54; Photodisc: 22, 36; Jeffrey L. Rotman: 15, 21, 63, 66; Tom Stack & Associates: 39 (Jeff Foott), 41 (Brian Parker); Tom & Therisa Stack/Tom Stack & Associates: 58, 65; VWPICS.com: 30 (Villoch), 77 (P. Parks – I3D); James Watt/Animals Animals/Earth Scenes: 37, 40, 87; Ralph White/Corbis: 17, 75, 76; E. Widder/HBOI/Visuals Unlimited: 16, 68.

[LIBRARY OF CONGRESS CATALOGING-IN-PUBLICATION DATA]
CIP data available

Table of Contents

Chapter One

Defining Oceans and Seas

❧ Sometime in the distant past, humans decided to venture onto the oceans. They went out to sea first in rafts, then in flimsy wooden boats. Over time, brave sailors sailed

farther away from land. Many ships never returned.

Wise men thought about the lost ships. They came up with two possibilities. First, they thought some ships may have reached the ocean's edge and fallen off. Second, they believed hideous sea monsters may have swallowed ships whole.

Ancient maps tell us what people believed long ago. Mapmakers of Christopher Columbus's day drew the ocean's edge for sailors to avoid. They also pinpointed locations of sea dragons. These sites were labeled "Here, there be monsters."

Today, ships sail without fear of falling off the edge of the oceans. But the monster situation is less clear. The ocean holds creatures beyond the imagination:

- A dead giant squid was found in New Zealand waters in 1996. It measured 26 feet (8 meters) in length. That may seem enormous, but the longest squid ever found was twice that size!

- The bell of an Arctic giant jellyfish can measure 7 feet (2.1 m) across. The **tentacles** of some stretch more than 100 feet (30.5 m) long.

- Conger eel **larvae** begin life at a little more than 1 inch (2.54 centimeters) long. They reach 9 feet (2.75 m)

> **?** **WORDS TO KNOW . . .**
>
> **larvae (LAR-vee)** insects at the stage of development between eggs and pupae when they look like worms
>
> **tentacles (TEN-tuh-kuhlz)** the long, thin body parts of an animal that are used to hold, grab, or touch

◄ In the days of Christopher Columbus, most people believed the seas were filled with monsters.

▲ From space, it is obvious that the earth is a watery world.

as adults. Scientists once saw eel larvae about 6 feet (1.8 m) long living on the ocean floor. They wondered how big that adult eel would grow! Some people call earth the third rock from the sun. But earth is really more like a puddle than a rock. Nearly 71 percent of earth is covered with water. Of that water, 97 percent fills the oceans, seas, bays, and gulfs. The rest exists as lakes, rivers, glaciers, and ice caps, or it is underground.

The Oceans

🦎 Earth has five major oceans: the Pacific, Atlantic, Indian, Arctic, and Southern (Antarctic). Although all the oceans are connected, they each have unique species and features found nowhere else on earth. The Pacific and Atlantic

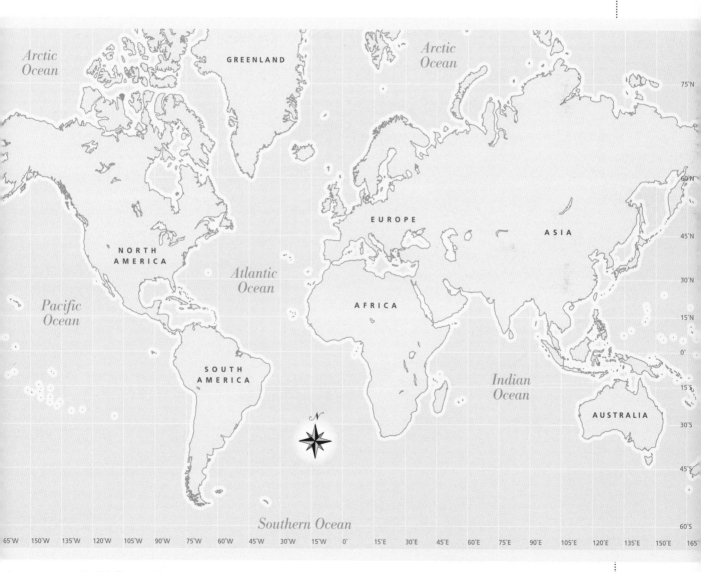

▲ Earth's five major oceans

❓ WORDS TO KNOW . . .

reef (REEF) a shallow strip of rock, sand, or coral in the ocean or another body of water

trench (TRENCH) a deep canyon on the ocean floor

have north and south regions, divided by the equator.

The Pacific Ocean holds about half of earth's water. It is the largest, deepest ocean. The world's deepest **trench,** highest mountain, and longest **reef** all lie in the Pacific. Earth's deepest point is 36,198 feet (11,033 m) under the ocean and is called the Challenger Deep of the Mariana Trench. The highest mountain is Hawaii's Mauna Loa, which rises about 56,000 feet (17,000 m) from the seafloor. Mount Everest, earth's highest mountain measured

from sea level (as opposed to seafloor), reaches only 29,035 feet (8,850 m) in height! And no reef compares with the Great Barrier Reef. It stretches about 1,240 miles (2,000 kilometers) along the northeast coast of Australia.

The Atlantic Ocean is second in size and also has its share of interesting features. The Mid-Atlantic Ridge runs for 6,215 miles (10,000 km) down the ocean's center, along the seafloor. It is earth's longest mountain range.

Continents rest on large, slowly moving parts of earth's crust called plates. Two major plates touch at the Mid-Atlantic Ridge. As the plates move away from each other, the seafloor spreads apart. It separates at

▲ Dramatic tides change the beach profile in the Bay of Fundy, Canada.

a rate of about 1 inch (2.54 cm) a year.

The Atlantic also claims the world's greatest tidal change. Tourists flock to the Bay of Fundy, Nova Scotia, Canada, to see the changing tides. Water in the Bay of

◄ Australia's Great Barrier Reef is an ancient and extensive coral reef habitat.

Fundy shifts about 48 feet (15 m) on average between low and high tide.

The Indian Ocean borders Africa's eastern coast and the coast of southern Asia, and then curls in a C shape around Australia. The Ninety East Ridge runs north to south in the Indian Ocean. It is a series of underwater peaks that form a nearly straight line along the **longitude** line at 90°E.

The Indian Ocean provides a safe haven for a fish called the coelacanth. In 1938, fishers pulled up their catch and found a coelacanth in their nets. Until that day, this fish was believed to be **extinct.** Since 1938, a number of coelacanths have been found living in the Indian Ocean. Scientists believe that about 200 coelacanths live in underwater caves off the Comoros Islands, near Madagascar, Africa.

The Arctic and Southern (Antarctic) Oceans are near earth's poles. Their waters are very cold, yet filled with life. The largest population of krill, the favorite food of **baleen** whales, lies under the ice of the Southern Ocean.

▲ Scientists believed the coelacanth had been extinct for eons—until one was caught off the coast of South Africa.

▲ Thousands of icebergs create shipping hazards each year.

between 15,000 and 30,000 icebergs annually. Antarctica creates record-setting icebergs. In March 2000, an iceberg dropped off the Ross Ice Shelf, part of the Antarctic shelf. It measured just less than 6,200 square miles (16,000 sq km), or about the size of Connecticut and Rhode Island combined.

The Seas

There is some confusion over what is and what is not a sea. The word *sea* can be a synonym for *ocean*. Seas are also large bodies of water partially enclosed by land. Every ocean has seas near landmasses. Major world seas include the Caribbean, Mediterranean,

Glaciers and sea ice occur in both polar regions. When edges of glaciers break off at the shore, they make icebergs by the thousands. The Arctic Ocean averages

Bering, Red, North, and the South China seas.

Some seas are called gulfs or bays, such as the Gulf of Mexico or Hudson Bay. Other bodies of water are called seas but are really lakes because they have no ocean outlet. The Caspian and Aral seas are misnamed lakes.

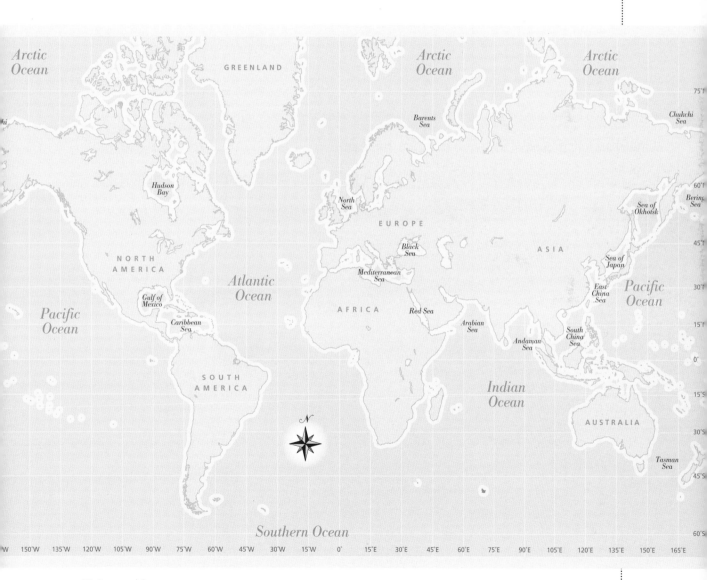

▲ Major world seas

? WORDS TO KNOW . . .

benthic (BEHN-thick) along the ocean floor

floes (FLOWZ) sheets of floating ice

haul out (HAWL OUT) move from the sea to the beach or to a location on the beach; walruses, seals, and sea lions will do this as a group

intertidal (IN-tur-TIE-duhl) of the area between the high and low tide marks on a beach

pelagic (peh-LAA-jick) of the top layers of open ocean, particularly the area that gets sun

One of the largest seas is the Bering Sea, which lies between Russia and the United States. Walruses compete for space on Bering Sea ice **floes.** Fur seals and sea lions **haul out** to breed on islands in the sea. Even polar bears find Bering Sea waters refreshing. Polar bears think nothing of a 50-mile (80-km) swim through ice-filled Bering Sea waters.

Who Lives Where

Oceans and seas have "living" zones where different species live. The regions include the **intertidal, pelagic,** and **benthic** zones. Few species cross from one zone to another.

▲ At low tide, these tide pools along the Oregon coast are exposed to the sun.

The intertidal zone lies along the coastline. High and low tides mark the range of this zone. On a rock-strewn beach, the intertidal zone might contain tide pools. Crabs, sea stars, snails, urchins, and barnacles live among varieties of seaweed in tide pools. Few plants live in the sandy intertidal zone. However, air bubbles in the sand show the hiding places of worms, clams, and tiny crabs. Birds such as gulls, terns, and sandpipers peck at the wet sand to find food.

The pelagic zone is the top layer of open ocean. The pelagic zone ranges from the surface to a dark zone. The most active region is the area with the most sunlight. This zone provides much of the

◀ Polar bears hunt ring seals on the Arctic ice pack.

seafood and fish that humans eat. Sunlight allows **photosynthesis** to take place. Green plants can survive by using **chlorophyll** and sunlight to make food and oxygen. **Marine** plants provide food and shelter for hundreds of ocean species. Plant eaters draw the attention of predators. The constant movement of sea life keeps the pelagic zone busy.

The benthic zone holds the mysteries of the deep sea. No sunlight reaches the benthic zone. Water pressure is strong enough to crush a human body flat. Creatures of the deep search the ocean floor for food that sinks from above.

Many deep-sea dwellers glow in the dark. Fish, squid, and tiny plants and animals create light just like lightning bugs. They use a chemical process called **bioluminescence** that makes sharks glow green and deep-sea shrimp appear bright red. Despite the darkness, the cold, and the

◀ A deep ocean anglerfish attracts prey with a lure that dangles in front of its face and lights up.

immense pressure, the benthic zone teems with life. It is home to crabs and tube worms. Some of the ugliest fish in the world live there, too!

The Ocean in Motion

🦎 The oceans and seas move constantly. Tides, currents, and waves create an ever-changing seascape. This motion plays an important role in the ocean cycle of life.

The sun and the moon cause the changes in water levels around earth. These changes are tides. The moon is much smaller than the sun, but closer to earth. It has more effect on earth's oceans than the sun does.

▲ Tubeworms live in the benthic zone— the deepest region of the ocean.

The moon has gravity, an invisible force that pulls toward the center of a body. The moon moves around earth, pulling on the water closest to it. The water swells

📖 **READ IT!**

Creatures of the Deep: In Search of the Sea's Monsters and the World They Live In by Erich Hoyt (Firefly Books, 2001) presents up close and personal views of some of the creepiest, strangest, and meanest-looking creatures in the oceans.

toward the moon, creating a high tide. On the opposite side of earth, another swell occurs. Two high tides occur each day, about 12 hours apart.

The sun's gravity also pulls on earth. It is farther away than the moon, so the pull is not as strong. When the sun and the moon line up on the same side of earth, they pull together. This creates very high tides, called spring tides. Sometimes the sun's and the

moon's positions form right angles to earth. When this happens, earth experiences lower, or neap, tides.

Currents

✒ All water in an ocean or sea does not move in the same direction or at the same speed. Water flows through the oceans like rivers. Currents are the ocean's rivers.

Both surface and under-water currents move ocean water. Surface currents are influenced by factors such as gravitational forces and wind patterns. The wind pushes the water in the same direction as it is blowing.

Surface currents can be either cold or warm water currents. The Kamchatka,

▲ Wind and gravitational forces drive ocean currents.

Labrador, and Humboldt currents carry cold water from polar seas toward the equator. The Gulf Stream, East Australia, and Equatorial currents carry warm water away from the equator.

Most surface currents move slowly at up to 5 miles (8 km) daily. They follow a regular pattern that can be

◄ The moon's gravity pulls ocean water, producing high and low tides.

mapped. The Kuroshio Current and the Gulf Stream are ocean speed demons. They move at rates up to 75 miles (121 km) per day.

Underwater currents move frigid water along the ocean's floor. The largest deep ocean current is the Pacific Deep Western Boundary Current.

▲ Charted ocean and sea currents

▲ Although it seems hard and crusty, coral is actually a community of living creatures.

This current flows north from the Southern Ocean along eastern New Zealand. It carries about 100 times as much water as the Amazon or the Nile, which are the earth's longest rivers.

Currents carry tiny plants and animals in ocean water.

Animals attached to rocks (barnacles or mussels) or to the seafloor (anemones or coral) depend on currents to bring them food. Currents also attract schooling fish such as cod, haddock, or pollock that feed on smaller fish. Even whales take part in the all-you-can-eat buffet offered by major ocean currents.

Waves

Waves move water from the open ocean toward the shore. Wind produces most waves. The area of water affected by a body of wind is called the fetch. Wind blows across the fetch, causing water to rise into waves. A profile of a wave shows a high spot (the crest) and a low spot (the trough). If a weather report describes waves of 10 to 12 feet (3 to 3.7 m), 10 feet (3 m) is the distance between the wave's crest and trough. Because wind does not blow with the same strength at all times, waves vary in height.

▲ This is all that was left after this community was struck by a tsunami.

Underwater events also cause waves. Earthquakes, volcanoes, and landslides on the ocean floor produce energy under the water. The energy pushes the water up into waves. Earthquakes can cause tsunamis (soo-NAH-meez), or giant waves. An earthquake in Peru can generate a tsunami strong enough to travel across the Pacific Ocean and hit Japan. Four-fifths of all tsunamis occur in the Pacific.

Waves act like blenders along the coast. They churn up the ocean floor. Wave action shifts beach sand and underwater sand. Waves change the profile of a beach and the position of sandbars. When they do so, they change the habitats of millions of plants and animals.

> **! WOULD YOU BELIEVE?**
>
> One of the world's largest recorded tsunamis struck Lituya Bay, Alaska, in 1958. The wave reached more than 1,700 feet (518 m) high. That is more than 250 feet (76 m) taller than the Sears Tower in Chicago, Illinois.

◄ Whales travel in groups called pods. These whales are performing a common activity, called breaching.

2

Focus on Reefs and Key Species

Scuba divers float in the shallow waters of the Great Barrier Reef. The water is clear, warm, and inviting. The divers watch brilliant crimson-and-white clownfish dart

among the coral **polyps** below. This, and every other coral reef, began with just one polyp anchored to the seafloor.

Coral comes in strange shapes and beautiful colors. Bright red fire coral grows beside green, leaflike cabbage coral. Lacy fan coral hides a seahorse. Nearby, an octopus buries itself beneath a mound of brain coral.

Hard coral leaves a skeleton when it dies. The skeleton becomes part of a coral reef. Soft coral looks much like seaweed or anemones. Coral colors cover the rainbow, from deep purples and spinach greens to vivid reds, pinks, and yellows.

Reef-building coral is a keystone species of the ocean.

▲ A healthy coral reef has as much traffic as a big city during rush hour.

Keystone species make such an impact on an **ecosystem** that the ecosystem cannot survive without them. Coral reefs change the ocean environment. Hundreds of plant

? WORDS TO KNOW . . .

ecosystem (EE-koh-siss-tuhm) a community of plants and animals and their relationship with the surrounding environment

polyps (POL-ips) small sea animals with tube-shaped bodies and tentacles

◂ Red polyp coral is noted for its stunning scarlet color.

▲ Mangrove swamps serve as nurseries for many ocean species.

👁 WATCH IT!

The Great Barrier Reef video
(ASIN: 158448134X) reveals the
colorful, dynamic, and fragile
life of animals on the world's
largest coral reef.

❓ WORDS TO KNOW . . .

biome (BYE-ohm) a large ecosystem in which the plants and animals are adapted to a particular
climate or physical environment

and animal species depend on the coral reef for food and shelter.

Many different keystone species affect the ecosystems in the ocean **biome.** Some live in coastal zones, others in the open sea. Let's consider groups of keystone species such as krill and plankton, sea otters, kelp, and mangrove trees. They are all groups of keystone species that live in the ocean, yet there is not one fish among them!

The word *plankton* covers a large number of small marine beings. Plant plankton (phytoplankton) and animal plankton (zooplankton) survive by floating through the ocean. They move on currents, tides, and waves.

Some phytoplankton are small, one-celled, and round like a ball. This shape helps some phytoplankton float. Zooplankton range from one-celled animals to krill and jellyfish. Every ocean animal depends on plankton. They either eat plankton directly or eat creatures that consume plankton.

Mangroves and kelp also serve as groups of keystone species. The mangrove is an odd tree. It grows along tropical shorelines and survives in both freshwater and salt water. The trunks and branches grow above the waterline. The roots form a weblike network under the water. Young fish, turtles, and reptiles thrive in their mangrove nursery.

KRILL IN THE NEWS

In March 2002, a group of British scientists made a fascinating discovery. Their robot submarine discovered huge amounts of krill living under the ice in Antarctica. The Antarctic krill had five times as many individuals per area than krill in open waters.

The krill feed along the underside of sea ice during winter months. Dr. Andrew Brierley, of the scientific team, said the discovery was of major importance because "it shows that it is the ice edge, rather than sea ice generally, that is important for krill."

▲ Kelp forests protect small fish and sea creatures from larger predators.

📖 READ IT!

Threatened Oceans by Jenny Tesar (Facts On File, 1991) gives a true picture of the environmental problems damaging the oceans.

roots, called holdfasts, cling to the seafloor. Kelp can grow up to about 200 feet (61 m) long. An air sac at the tip of each frond holds the kelp upright in the water. Kelp forests house 800 different plant and animal species.

Kelp forests and sea otters share a close relationship. Without sea otters eating urchins, the kelp forest would die. Urchins chew on kelp holdfasts. Eventually, they chew through the base, and the frond floats away. Kelp forests support hundreds of species, and the sea otter, in turn, preserves the kelp forest.

Kelp forests lie mostly underwater. The beds may become exposed at low tide. Kelp is a form of brown algae, or seaweed. Kelp

Umbrella Species

🐇 Protecting an umbrella species requires protecting

▲ A gray whale cow and her calf head north to the Arctic. The calf stretched nearly 16 feet (4.9 m) at birth.

territory. An umbrella species is a plant or animal that, when protected, also protects other species. For example, Pacific gray whales migrate along the West Coast of North America. Their territory extends from the Arctic Ocean to Baja, California. If the gray whales' territory is protected from net fishing during migration, other marine animals living there are also protected.

Corals can also be umbrella species. A protected reef includes algae, anemones, and reef-dwelling creatures. It also safeguards "visitors" to the reef, such as sharks and rays.

Green sea turtles serve as umbrella species in sea grass

▲ Batlike manta rays are filter feeders, surviving on plankton and shrimp.

beds. Green sea turtles groom sea grass beds, keeping the grasses and reeds healthy. Laws preserve both the turtles and the sea grass beds. Doing so provides a safe haven for manatees, sharks, rays, and dozens of fish species.

Flagship Species

A flagship species brings people's attention to a biome. It is easy to interest people in efforts to "Save the Whales" or "Save the Dolphins." Both species have drama, intelligence, and personality. However, few people sign up to "Save the Sea Cucumber" or "Save the Portuguese Man-of-War." Though these species lack popularity, they still need protecting.

Flagship species represent the brightest, most beautiful, and most enchanting creatures of a biome. They are valuable to the biome, as well. Efforts to conserve flagship species make people more aware of the problems of the whole ecosystem.

Here's an example. For many years, dolphins were **by-catch** of tuna fisheries. Dolphins got caught in tuna nets and drowned. An outraged public supported the dolphins, and ways were

---

✋ DO IT!

If ecology interests you, join the Kids Ecology Corps. It's free! Access information about the corps at *http://www.kidsecology.org.*

❓ WORDS TO KNOW . . .

by-catch (BYE-kach) fish, turtles, or mammals caught by accident while nets fish for specific species, such as tuna

▲ Sleek dolphins used high-pitched sounds to locate schools of fish for dinner.

found to prevent many dolphin deaths. In the 1970s, nearly 200,000 dolphins died as by-catch each year. Today, that number is down to about 2,000 in U.S. waters.

Dolphins aren't the only species helped by better fishing methods. This effort also saved sea turtles, whales, seals, sea lions, and otters. By-catch victims are surviving because many people are willing to pay a little more for canned "dolphin-safe" tuna in order to save the dolphins.

Indicator Species

🦎 Indicator species measure the health of a region or ecosystem. If local fish are found floating belly up, there's something wrong. Sometimes, humans create the problems, such as **pollution** or oil spills. Other problems arise because of weather or natural changes in the environment.

The Ocean Alliance, a conservation group, uses sperm whales as an indicator species for the health of earth's oceans. Sperm whales can be found in every ocean.

PROFILE: EL NIÑO

El Niño occurs when seawater near the equator in the eastern Pacific becomes warmer than normal. El Niño affects weather patterns and sea life throughout the world. It is responsible for especially heavy rainfall in some places and drought in others.

In California's Channel Islands, seals and sea lions feed in the kelp forests. A recent occurrence of El Niño brought changes in water temperature, which reduced the animal population in the kelp beds. Reduced populations meant reduced food and starvation for many marine mammals.

Learn more about how El Niño affects the ocean at the Marine Mammal Center's Web site: *http://www.tmmc.org/learning/comm/el_nino_2002.asp*.

? WORDS TO KNOW . . .

pollution (puh-LOO-shuhn) the act of soiling or dirtying an environment

33

▲ Sperm whales are an indicator species of the oceans. Scientists can check a dead sperm whale's blubber for poison levels.

They dive to great depths, so they can show problems in the upper (pelagic) or lower (benthic) ocean zones. If poisons collect in the oceans, those same poisons collect in whale fat called blubber. When a sperm whale dies, scientists can check how much poison is in the whale's blubber.

Predators

A massive male walrus heaves his nearly 4,000-pound (1,814-kilogram) body into the water. Awkward on land, walruses are excellent swimmers and divers. The male heads for the seafloor. He gently brushes the bottom with his tusks and whiskers. It is an odd hunting technique, but it is effective. The walrus finds clams, worms, and crabs beneath the seafloor muck. Like sharks and orcas, the walrus is a predator. He lives by hunting and eating other sea animals.

▲ Alaskan natives called the walrus *toothwalker*. These 2-ton creatures are awkward on land but are elegant in the water.

Animal life in the ocean can be divided into three basic groups: plankton, nekton, and benthos. Plankton are floaters or drifters that have little or no means of self-propulsion. Currents, tides, and waves move them from place to place. Nekton are swimmers that include marine mammals, such as whales, seals, sea lions, dolphins, and fish such as sharks, cod, haddock, and surgeonfish. Benthos are bottom-feeders, consisting of animals that are stuck to the bottom, such as clams, mussels, and abalone. Other bottom-feeders crawl or slither along the seafloor, such as sea cucumbers, crabs, and lobsters.

The marine food chain has both predators and prey. Each plays an important role in keeping the ocean's natural balance. Top predators, such as sperm whales, sharks, and orcas, belong to the nekton group. They hunt aggressively and successfully

◄ Yellow tang surgeonfish are among the rainbow-colored species that live on coral reefs.

because they can stalk and attack their prey.

Sharks find their meals by scent. They have a keen sense of smell that works over long distances and even determines direction. Sharks have two nostrils. When a scent arrives at one nostril before the other, the shark knows where its prey is located. Sharks also hear sound over long distances. Because sharks stalk wounded prey, good hearing helps. They pick up sounds of pain or distress over many miles.

Porpoises, dolphins, and toothed whales, such as sperm and pilot whales, have either little or no sense of smell. They locate their prey using sound. They have an excellent sense of **echolocation** that works like

▲ Great white sharks have attacked humans. They are fierce, dangerous predators.

sonar in a submarine. Sonar is a device that uses sound waves to locate underwater objects. A pilot whale sends out a series of clicks. The clicks strike objects in the ocean and bounce back to the whale. Using echolocation, whales can figure

> **?** WORDS TO KNOW . . .
>
> echolocation (EK-oh-loh-kay-shuhn) the process of finding an object by bouncing sound off it to determine its size and distance; used by bats, whales, and dolphins

▲ It is common for dolphins to herd their prey into a bait ball.

! **WOULD YOU BELIEVE?**

Killer whales, also called orcas, are not whales at all. They are the largest species of dolphins. They are also the fastest dolphins, swimming at speeds up to 30 miles (48 km) per hour.

out the size, shape, distance, texture, direction, and speed of an object.

Dolphins and orcas hunt in groups to find, control, and capture their prey. Dolphins along the South Carolina coast herd fish onto sandy banks. The dolphins wiggle onto the bank, eat their catch, and return to the hunt. Dolphins also force small fish, such as herring or anchovies, into "bait balls." When the dolphins find a school of

A hungry orca prepares to catch this young sea lion. ▶

small fish, they attack from several sides. One dolphin emits a series of bubbles that frightens the prey. Small fish huddle in a ball by instinct. This "bait ball" makes feeding easy for the dolphins.

Orcas also use echolocation to identify prey. They hunt everything from seal pups to large whales. A group, or pod, of orcas hunts a female gray whale and her calf. The mother is too large, but the calf makes excellent prey. The orcas attack and retreat repeatedly. They force the calf underwater where it cannot breathe.

When hunting seals or sea lions, the orcas lurk in the breaking waves. The seals and sea lions must come into the water to find food. Orcas are waiting.

▲ Whale sharks are the largest fish, but, like many whales, they feed on plankton and krill.

Filter Feeders

🐟 Filter feeders take a milder approach to hunting. They simply swim through swarms of tiny prey and sift their food from what they don't want to eat. Filter feeders include baleen whales (blue, bowhead, finback, right, gray, minke, and humpback), whale sharks, basking sharks, and manta rays.

The blue whale is the largest marine mammal. In fact, it is the largest animal that has ever lived. Blue whales can grow more than 100 feet (30 m) long and can weigh up to 300,000 pounds

Beware the sea nettle. Its stinging tentacles inflict extreme pain. ▶

(136,100 kg). What is most amazing about blue whales is that they reach this size on a diet of krill (average length: 1 inch, or 2.54 cm).

Whale sharks are the largest fish in the oceans. They are not whales, just very large sharks. Whale sharks are filter feeders, just like baleen whales. Their open mouths take in huge amounts of ocean water, krill, plankton, and small fish.

Hide and Seek

Some predators wait for prey to come to them. They patiently float along. Some use camouflage. They hide behind

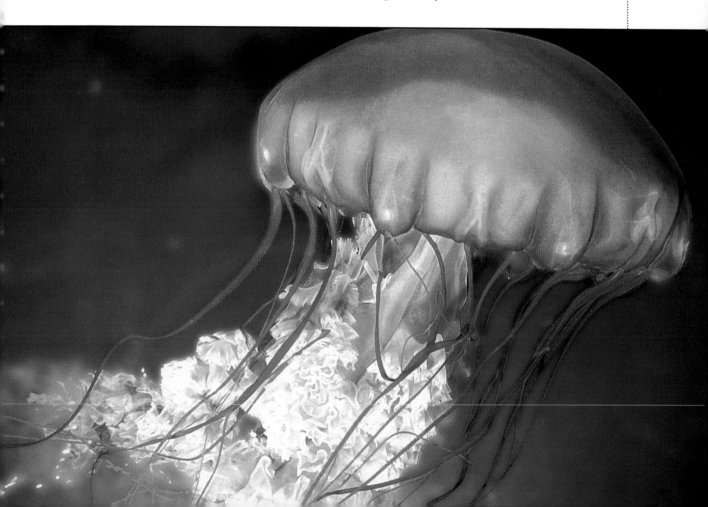

or under seafloor plants or rocks. For both kinds of predators, a meal eventually arrives.

Jellyfish and the Portuguese man-of-war eat plankton. They drift along waiting for prey. A jelly's medusa, or bell, contains the animal's main organs. Long, poisonous tentacles trail behind them. Large jellyfish, such as the Arctic giant or lion's mane, eat thousands of tiny plankton and fish eggs every day.

A Portuguese man-of-war, also known as the bluebottle, is actually a colony of individual polyps. The body consists of a float, organs, and tentacles. The float is a gas-filled bubble that is carried along the water's surface. A man-of-war's tentacles also sting and paralyze prey.

Other predators use camouflage. Most flat fish, such as flounder and plaice, have learned to bury themselves under loose seafloor sand. Their coloring blends in with the multicolored sand. They are in a perfect spot to

◄ Creatures are drawn to the deadly Portuguese man-of-war because of its bright, shiny appearance.

▲ The octopus is a master of disguise. It can hide in cracks along a reef or match its coloring with the sea floor.

wait for prey. Spotted scorpion fish look like rocks until their prey swims near. Then they attack.

A master of oceanic hide-and-seek is the octopus. Flexible and agile, the octopus slips under rocks, in cracks, or in a gravel nest. Its coloring matches its hiding place. When lobsters, crabs, or shrimp scurry past, the octopus pulls them in with its tentacles.

PROFILE: LEOPARD SEALS

Leopard seals are large mammals that prefer living alone. Females are slightly larger than males and can be 12 feet (3.7 m) long and up to 1,000 pounds (454 kg).

Leopard seals often eat krill but would rather feast on penguins. The seals lurk near Antarctic ice, waiting for penguins to plunge into the water. Nervous penguins are aware of the leopard seal's presence. They avoid diving in as long as they can, but hunger wins out. The seal attacks, but penguins are good swimmers. The penguins escape about half the time.

From Beyond the Sea

Many of the sea's most successful hunters are not fish. They are marine mammals, such as seals, sea lions, and walruses. Or, they are seabirds, such as penguins, albatross, and puffins.

Seals and sea lions are clumsy on land, yet are sleek and skilled in the water. Their fat layer of blubber and thick fur keep them warm in icy Arctic and Antarctic waters. Most seals and sea lions eat large amount of krill, fish, and squid.

Seabirds live extraordinary lives. Albatross, murres, and puffins live on the water and return to land only to breed. Penguins thrive in tempera-

Eighteen species of penguins live in ▶ the Antarctic. The largest are king penguins and emperor penguins.

tures colder than humans can survive. Pelicans, gulls, and terns choose homes with ocean views. These birds all have one thing in common. They depend on the ocean for food.

Gulls and terns scavenge in the intertidal zone, looking for crabs, worms, and small **crustaceans.** They can be seen on nearly every shoreline.

? WORDS TO KNOW . . .

crustaceans (kruhss-TAY-shuhnz)
animals with hard outside shells, such as crabs

▲ The puffin's bright orange beak makes it an odd-looking bird.

They also hunt at sea, plucking small fish from the water's surface. Even far out to sea, albatross, puffins, frigate birds, and shearwaters can hunt, easily scooping small fish from schools swimming along the surface.

Chapter Four

Prey

A school of anchovies swims just below the water's surface. A flock of shearwaters flying overhead catches the silver sparkle of the anchovies. The shearwaters barely skim the waves in their rush to reach the school. Shearwaters are daring fliers and skilled divers. They soar high, and then plunge 20 feet (6 m) into the Atlantic Ocean. Hundreds of shearwaters attack a school with millions of anchovies. If the prey's numbers were not so great, this species could not survive.

There are thousands, maybe millions, of predators

▲ The shearwater earns its name from its graceful flight just above the water's edge.

▲ One gray whale will eat 390,000 pounds (177,000 kg) of amphipods between late spring and early fall.

stalking the seas. Billions, perhaps trillions, of animals feed those predators. Huge populations of prey keep a balance in the ocean ecosystem.

Consider the gray whale and the **amphipod,** its favorite food. Pacific gray whales feed in the Bering or Chukchi Sea for five months, from late spring to early fall. During that time, one gray whale eats about 390,000 pounds (177,000 kg) of amphipods.

Krill serves as the main meal for baleen whales, dolphins, squid, seals, herring, and penguins. In fact, scientists estimate that the world's penguins and other seabirds eat 39,000,000 tons of krill yearly.

Small fish, such as sprats, anchovies, and herring, travel in huge schools. They swim the open seas and have little protection from predators. For them, the only chance of survival is their huge population.

Plankton

❧ The word *plankton* comes from the Greek word *planktos*, which means "wandering." Plankton, which include animals and plants, don't wander as much as they drift. When speaking of prey, however, *plankton* refers to zooplankton, which are floating animals.

Zooplankton include the protozoa, eggs, and young of larger animals. One type of

Schools of Pacific herring feed ▶ dolphins, seals, and larger fish.

plankton includes a variety of crustaceans with names that end in *pod*: copepods, amphipods, isopods, and decapods. *Pod* means "foot," and these mini-animals come with plenty of feet. There may be 10,000 different species of copepods. They are the most plentiful "pod" in the oceans. On average, 1 ounce (28.3 grams) of copepods includes 250 individuals.

Jellyfish are larger plankton. They can push themselves along, but usually they just drift with the currents. The Australian box jellyfish and the Portuguese man-of-war can be dangerous to humans. Encounters with box jellies may end in death if not treated immediately.

Spikes, Poison, and Hidey-Holes

For a sea creature to reach adulthood, it must not be eaten. This is not as simple as it sounds. It requires a combination of luck and good defenses. Defenses may be a prey's spines, spikes, stingers, hard shells, poisons, **toxic** mucus, or color or size changes. When these defenses fail, prey can either run or hide.

Spines, stingers, and spikes fend off all but the bravest predators. Coral and anemones use stinging

WATCH IT!

The Blue Planet, Seasonal Seas (ASIN: B00005YU7M) investigates the effect of plankton on their environment. When plankton spawn, sharks, jellyfish, rays, squid, and a host of fish species show up for the feast. Plankton may be small, but *Seasonal Seas* captures the tiniest details on video.

? WORDS TO KNOW . . .

toxic (TOK-sik) poisonous

◀ Tiny Daphnia copepods are also called water fleas.

51

COMB JELLYFISH IN THE NEWS

A type of comb jellyfish has taken over the Black Sea and the Caspian Sea. This may sound silly, but comb jellyfish spell disaster for fishers.

The jellies have no natural predators in the Black or Caspian seas. They do, however, have hefty appetites and eat everything they can. A typical diet includes zooplankton and fish eggs. The comb jellies' eating habits have reduced the fish population in the Black Sea by 80 percent. A similar problem is happening in the Caspian Sea.

Some scientists hope to combat the comb jellies with butterfish. Butterfish eat their own weight in comb jellies every hour. The comb jelly situation shows what happens when nature's balance is disturbed.

tentacles, urchins use spines, and sponges use chemical secretions to stop hungry enemies. Coral and anemones also use poison as a defense. Stingers can deliver enough poison to paralyze or kill a predator.

Many ocean animals survive because of their hard shells. Shrimp, crabs, lobsters, clams, and mussels have hard outer shells that protect them from many, but not all, predators. Some creatures, such as hermit crabs, borrow the shell of another animal such as a snail. Hermit crabs move into larger shells as they grow. Hermit crabs sometimes fight over quality shells.

Other plants and animals make themselves unappetizing to predators. They emit poison

▲ Multicolored parrotfish protect themselves at night by covering their bodies with toxic mucus.

or give off a bad-tasting substance. Parrotfish cover their bodies with toxic mucus when resting. Toxic substances work like insect repellent. Predators taste or smell the repellent and stay away.

One species uses just about every trick in the book.

Puffer fish have sharp, irritating spines. They bloat themselves up to appear too big for eating. They taste horrible and carry poison in their bodies. Finally, they bite with sharp teeth. No

📖 READ IT!

Reef Life by Denise Nielson-Tackett and Larry Tackett (Microcosm LTD, 2002) provides an in-depth, full-color view of coral ecosystems. Learn how plant and animal species survive amid constant threats in the eat-or-be-eaten world of a coral reef.

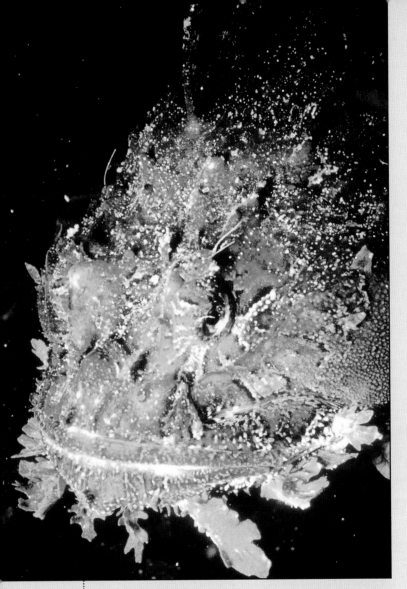

▲ The hideous scorpionfish hides in seaweed while it waits for its prey to pass by.

among the poison tentacles of a Portuguese man-of-war. They are immune to the poison, but their predators are not. Damselfish and clown fish rarely leave the safety of an anemone's poisonous tentacles.

When nothing else works, hiding provides some level of protection. The ocean floor contains many cracks, jutting rocks, holes, and caves where prey can hide. Eels and crabs scuttle under rocks when not feeding. Some creatures, such as the pipefish or the seahorse, blend in with plants or coral. Flounder, scorpion fish, and lizardfish hide on gravelly or sandy seafloors. They become nearly invisible against the seafloor—as long as they don't move.

sensible predator would bother with the puffer fish.

Sometimes, survival depends on help from other species. A few species of fish, including the jack fish, live

Chapter Five

Flora

❧ Marine flora, or sea plants, produce 90 percent of the oxygen on earth. Sea plants fall into two categories: phytoplankton and seaweed, which includes algae and sea grasses. Without marine flora, life on earth would end. Sea plants are the basic stuff of life.

Phytoplankton are one-celled, tiny plants that make up most of ocean plant life. These tiny plants live in the upper (pelagic) ocean zone,

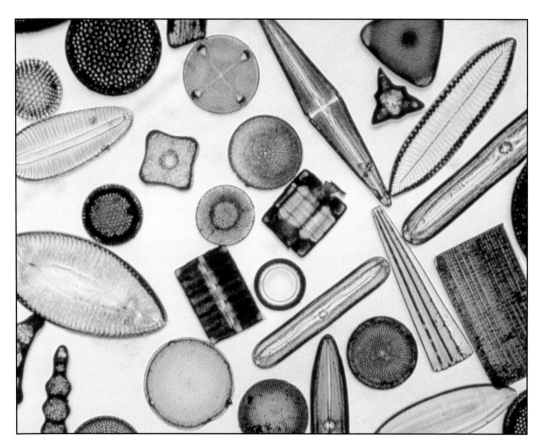

▲ Diatoms are living plants that drift on open seas.

▲ Even the harsh Arctic Ocean blooms with phytoplankton once winter ice melts.

DO IT!

Next time you go to the beach, collect a jar of seawater. Back at home, look at drops of the water through a microscope. You'll be surprised at what's living in your jar!

where there is plenty of sunlight. In warm, clear ocean water, phytoplankton grow to depths of about 400 feet (122 m). Phytoplankton drift through the water. They provide food for thousands of animal species.

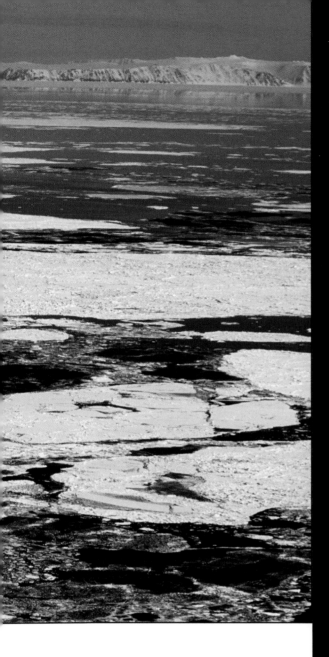

Even the Arctic Ocean has its share of phytoplankton. During icy winter months, the phytoplankton stay inactive. When the

ALIEN INVADES MEDITERRANEAN!

In the 1970s, the Wilhelmina Zoo in Stuttgart, Germany, added *Caulerpa taxifola*, a delicate form of seaweed, to its tropical tanks. The zoo provided other public aquariums with samples of caulerpa. Their generosity sparked a nightmare.

Bits of caulerpa escaped from aquarium tanks. The seaweed made its way into the Mediterranean Sea. Caulerpa developed into a science-fiction monster.

Caulerpa does not belong in the Mediterranean. Mediterranean fish and sea creatures won't eat the toxic weed. Actually, they won't even touch it.

Mediterranean communities see disaster coming as the seaweed thrives. Caulerpa covers and kills other seaweed. It also kills off the animals that depend on native plants for survival. Salting, vacuuming, and pulling caulerpa out by the roots has no effect. Nothing kills the stuff. What will stop the dreaded caulerpa?

summer sun lights the Arctic sky for nearly 23 hours a day, the phytoplankton population booms.

Phytoplankton is invisible to the human eye. Yet, people who swim at night may notice a faint yellow-green glow on their skin. That is phytoplankton. Some of it glows in the dark.

Occasionally, the phytoplankton population explodes. This event is called a bloom.

It results from the ideal mix of light, warmth, and plant food. Blooms are visible to humans because the plants form a thick layer on the water.

Algae

🐟 Dabberlocks, bladder wrack, toothed wrack, and dulse. These sound like bizarre diseases or magical spells. Actually, they are types of seaweed. More correctly, they are large, colored forms of algae. Common seaweed comes in green, brown, or red. Some drift on the tides. Other seaweed use holdfasts to anchor themselves to the seafloor.

Green seaweed grows in most oceans. Typical examples are sea lettuce, sea grass, eelgrass, and caulerpa. Some northern European cultures eat sea lettuce in salads. It is easy to harvest because sea lettuce grows in tide pools.

Kelp, wrack, dabberlocks, and oarweed are types of brown seaweed. Kelp grows in underwater forests along the coast. Most people eat kelp daily without realizing it. Kelp appears in ice cream, toothpaste, and salad dressings, and can even be eaten raw in salads. Wrack is a common brown seaweed that floats with the help of air

👁 **WATCH IT!**

Into the Deep (ASIN: B0000687MT) is a video that explores the kelp beds of California's Channel Islands. Learn about fierce Garibaldi fish, Spanish mackerel, and dozens of other species that call the kelp forest home.

◄ Bladder wrack is a type of brown seaweed used to make plant fertilizer.

bladders. Types of wrack include knotted, spiral, toothed, bladder, and channeled. Wrack makes excellent natural fertilizer.

Red algae has long been popular in preparing different kinds of food. The form called Irish moss, or carrageenan, thickens pudding, soups, and cream cheese. Dulse, another red seaweed, is used in both food and medicine. Dulse attaches itself to rocks in the North Atlantic and Northwest Pacific oceans. As far back as the days of the Vikings, people have eaten highly nutritious dulse. Snails, urchins, and small, shell-covered animals called limpets like it, too.

PROFILE: THE SARGASSO SEA

Tiny shrimp, worms, and infant sea turtles find safe haven in the Sargasso Sea. This is not a true sea but a large area of floating seaweed. Air sacs keep the seaweed afloat. The Sargasso Sea is found in the Atlantic Ocean near Bermuda.

Chapter Six

Herbivores

A green turtle munches on eelgrass growing in a quiet Brazilian bay. She weeds out dying blades of grass and keeps the eelgrass bed healthy. As a **hatchling,** she ate shrimp, crabs, and jellyfish.

As an adult, she eats only plants. In fact, the green sea turtle is the only plant eater among sea turtles.

Herbivore comes from the Latin words *herb,* meaning "plant," and *vore,* meaning "eater." Many of the largest land animals

? WORDS TO KNOW . . .

hatchling (HACH-ling) young that has just hatched from an egg

▲ A female green turtle swims past a bed of coral.

▲ Kelp is a large form of algae—the green stuff that coats home aquariums.

are herbivores. They include elephants, giraffes, buffalo, and rhinoceroses. In the oceans, green sea turtles and sea cows (dugongs and manatees) are the only large plant eaters.

Ocean herbivores live in the pelagic and intertidal zones. That's where marine plants grow. Algae and phytoplankton need sunlight, just like oak trees and grass. As the ocean gets deeper, colder, and darker, fewer plants are found. In very deep water, there are no plants and no plant eaters.

One-celled ocean plants provide food for zooplankton.

Copepods eat the most plants because there are more copepods than any other zooplankton. Both copepods and phytoplankton drift on the seas. Other animals, such as clams or mussels, filter the plankton from the moving water. They eat balanced meals of meat (zooplankton) and vegetables (phytoplankton).

Tide pools form on rocky shores. Seaweed clings to the rocks as waves batter the tide pools. Tide pools house several plant eaters. Limpets thrive in tide pools. They move over rocks and vacuum algae from the surface. Like snails, they leave a slime trail behind them.

Urchins live in tide pools, kelp beds, and coral reefs.

Urchins eat larger sea plants, such as wrack, dulse, and kelp. Colorful urchins protect themselves with sharp spines. They

Urchins feast on kelp. Sea otters feast on urchins. ▶
They are all part of the oceanic food cycle.

gnaw at kelp holdfasts and do serious damage to kelp beds. Luckily, sea otters, crabs, and wolf fish keep sea urchin populations under control.

Sea Cows

Manatees, dugongs, and Steller's sea cows, a now extinct species, belong to the same family of mammals, often called sea cows. They live in shallow, warm water with plenty of sea grass. They breathe air like dolphins and whales. However, their closest natural relative is the elephant!

Sea cows eat sea grass and flowering plants that grow in bays, such as hyacinths and hydrillas. They munch up to 100 pounds (45 kg) of plant matter daily.

PROFILE: COWRIES

Cowries are herbivores that graze on algae at night. They form remarkably beautiful shells. Their shells blend in with sand and gravel seafloors to protect cowries from predators.

In some countries, cowries have been used as money and made into jewelry. In Fiji and the Solomon Islands of the South Pacific, the golden cowrie is a sign of a tribal chief's power. Some people believe that cowries protect them from evil spells.

Pollution and the clearing of sea grass from rivers and bays has reduced the sea cows' food supply. These meek creatures are endangered throughout the world.

Balanced Nature

Coral reefs show how nature balances life in an ecosystem. Coral builds reefs in warm, shallow ocean water. Filter feeders, such as coral and anemones, keep the water clear.

Algae grow well in warm, shallow, clear water. In fact, algae could

LOOK IT UP!

The Save the Manatee Club is dedicated to preserving manatee habitats and keeping Florida's manatees safe. Learn more about manatees from the club's Web site: http://www.savethemanatee.org.

▲ Slow-moving manatees thrive in areas where sea grass is plentiful.

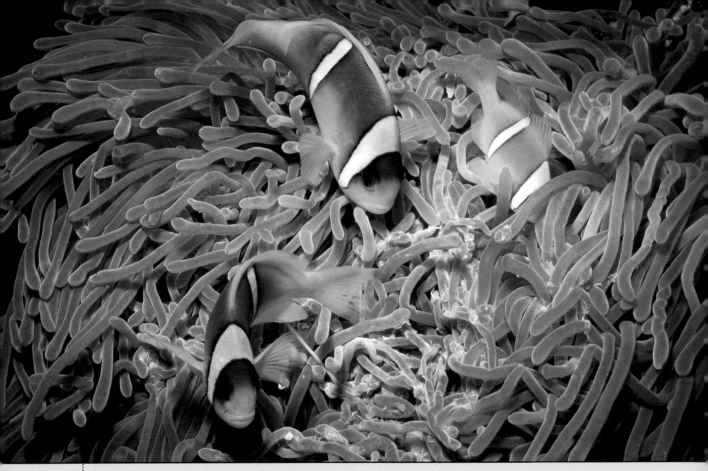

▲ Clownfish live comfortably among the poisonous tentacles of sea anemones. They are immune to the anemone's sting.

grow so quickly that it might cover up a reef. The coral would die. Nature balances plant and animal growth so both can live.

Many reef-dwelling fish are herbivores. Blue-and-purple parrot fish, dainty surgeonfish, and bold damselfish chew on algae vigorously to limit its growth. They protect coral from being overrun by algae. They live among the poisonous coral tentacles. The tentacles protect the fish from predators. The process of two living things working for each other's well-being is called symbiosis.

Chapter Seven

A Cycle of Life

☙ A male sperm whale dies. Like other whales, this male has played his part in preserving his species. He fathered more than three dozen calves during his life. His daughters and their offspring move in pods throughout the North Atlantic. His sons wait until they will be old enough to mate with females.

Sperm whales hunt the deep ocean for their food. They easily dive 4,000 feet (1,220 m) deep. Bottom-dwelling squid are a favorite food for sperm whales.

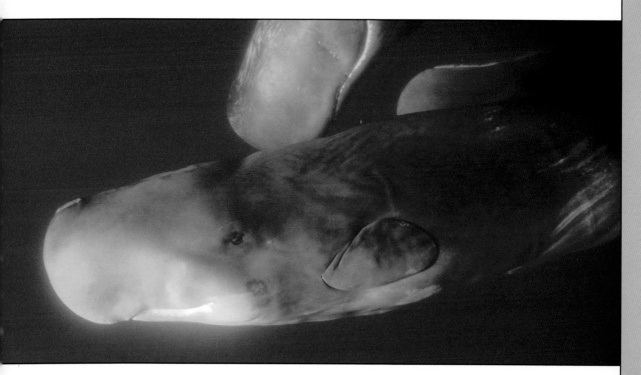

▲ Sperm whales can easily dive 4,000 feet (1,220 m) deep when hunting for squid.

Snapper, lobster, and an occasional shark round out the menu.

This male weighs in at about 80,000 pounds (36,288 kg). From blowhole to tail, he measures nearly 60 feet (18 m). Upon his death, the whale sinks to the ocean floor. There, he plays out his final role in the ocean cycle of life.

The first creatures to reach the sperm whale's corpse are amphipods. These tiny shrimplike creatures live in the muck on the ocean floor. They swarm across the whale **carcass.**

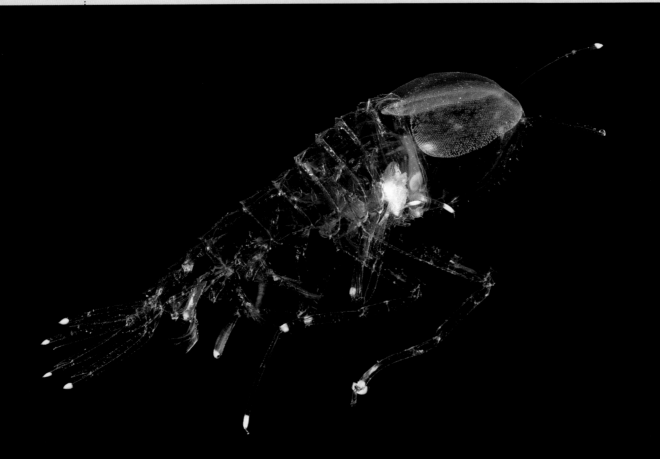

The scent of death travels quickly through the water. Within a short time, hagfish and rat-tails arrive. Both fish are scavengers, scouring the seafloor for food. Hagfish and rat-tails will feed on the carcass until every edible bit is gone.

Hagfish look like eels or large worms. They have no teeth. Instead, hagfish bore into a carcass with their power-ful tongues and suck out the flesh. They tie their bodies into knots to press against their food source. This gives them extra power when suck-ing at tough meat.

Rat-tails are one of the most common fish species liv-ing on the ocean floor. Because food is scarce in their habitat, they eat anything. Rat-tails

▲ Hagfish rip the flesh from dead fish in the benthic zone.

have large heads with big, dark eyes. Their bodies taper to a narrow tail, giving them the name rat-tail.

Out of the murky water comes a form from prehistoric times—a bluntnose sixgill shark. The sharks have been drawn by the smell of death. These deep-sea sharks are

◄ A deep-sea amphipod eats carrion that drifts down to the sea floor.

PROFILE: DEEP-SEA SHARKS

About 350 shark species live in or travel in deep seas. They range from the exceptionally small pygmy or dwarf shark (10 inches or 25 cm) to the slow-moving sleeper or Greenland shark (23 feet or 7 m). Many deep-sea sharks glow in the dark. This bioluminescent ability makes them glow with an eerie greenish light.

The bluntnose sixgill shark is related to prehistoric sharks. It is grayish brown in color and grows to about 16 feet (4.9 m). The bluntnose swims in all oceans at depths reaching 5,900 feet (1,800 m).

The most common deep-water shark is the spiny dogfish shark. Also called the skittledog and the codshark, the dogfish shark may end up on your dinner table. Most shark meat sold in grocery stores is dogfish shark. Dogfish sharks are small, averaging about 3 to 4 feet (0.9 to 1.2 m) long. They live at depths of up to 2,400 feet (732 m).

more like their early ancestors than the modern sharks found in upper ocean waters. They gladly feed on corpses that drift down from above. Their teeth tear at the whale's flesh. Once full, they glide back into the darkness.

After nearly two years, the sperm whale's carcass is just a clutter of bones on the seafloor. Still, bones provide nutrition. Within months, clams, mussels, and worms take over where the hagfish, rat-tails, and sharks left off. They build colonies on the whale's bones.

A carcass does not fall to the seafloor every day. Bottom dwellers can't be picky eaters. They must eat everything. When they die, they, too, will become part of the ocean cycle of life. Their bodies will feed their neighbors in the dark ocean depths.

▲ This sixgill shark traces its ancestors back to prehistoric times.

[Chapter Eight]

Diving Deep

A two-person submarine rocks in the ocean waves. The clamp holding the sub to the research ship releases. Inside the sub, two scientists begin a journey only a few miles long. Their trip takes them to a world no one has ever seen before. They explore earth's final frontier—the deep ocean.

This trip took place in 1977. Robert Ballard and John Corliss squeezed into the *Alvin,* a two-person submarine. The sub traveled only 1.5 miles (2.4 km) to the Pacific Ocean floor. There, they found wonders beyond anything they had ever considered. In an article in *National Geographic* magazine, the two described what they had seen: "Shimmering water streams up past giant tube worms. . . . A crab scuttles over lava encrusted with limpets. . . . These vents, like lush oases in a sunless desert,

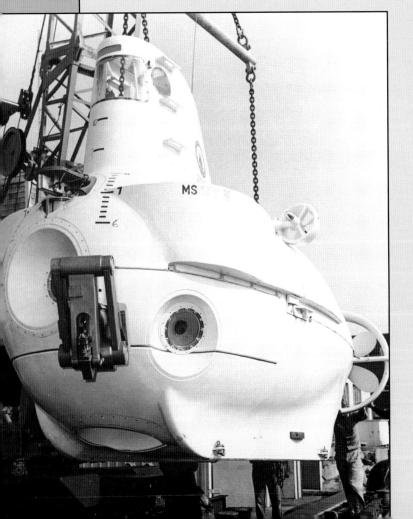

◀ The *Alvin* minisub took scientists on a journey into the deep ocean.

▲ Hot-water geysers, like Old Faithful in Yellowstone Park, also appear in the deep ocean.

are a phenomenon totally new to science."

Ballard and Corliss discovered a **hydrothermal** vent. Hot-water vents are underwater hot springs much like those found in Yellowstone National Park. The springs gush water at temperatures of 500° to 600° Fahrenheit (260° to 316° Celsius). The vent they discovered spewed water so hot

> **?** WORDS TO KNOW . . .
>
> **hydrothermal (HI-droh-THUR-muhl)** relating to hot water

▲ Volcanic action in the seas has built islands, like Iceland (shown here) and all of Hawaii.

that it melted the thermometers the scientists used to measure the heat.

The Deep Ocean Landscape

🦎 A side view of the ocean floor looks like land. There are mountains, plains, rolling hills, and deep valleys. The ocean landscape changes in the same way earth's surface changes. Volcanic eruptions build mountains, while earthquakes push and pull against earth's crust.

Scientists have known for a long time that volcanoes erupt underwater. Continued eruptions build islands and seamounts. Hawaii and Iceland are volcanic islands built by eruptions. Seamounts are

When deep-sea vents ooze dark chemical compounds, they are called smokers. ▶

underwater mountains. They are usually inactive, or dormant, volcanoes and are often cone-shaped. Seamounts rise 3,000 to 10,000 feet (914 to 3,050 m) from the ocean floor. Thousands of seamounts dot the seafloor landscape.

New Forms of Life

Deep-sea vents occur where the seafloor cracks open and exposes hot, liquid rock called lava. Super-heated water bursts into the deep ocean like black smoke. Many vents are called black smokers. Scientists discovered the first black smoker in 1977. The black water is not really smoking. It is especially salty and full

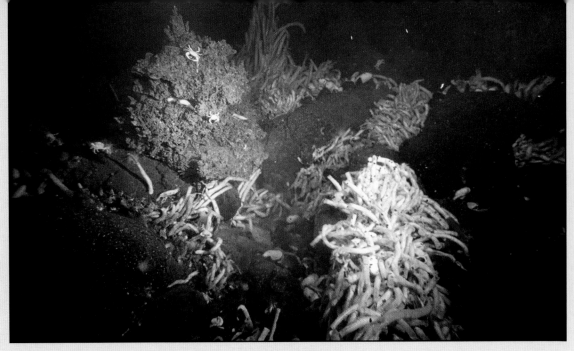

▲ Tubeworms and crabs survive near vents despite the lack of sunlight and oxygen.

of minerals, such as sulfur, iron, copper, zinc, and nickel. This mineral "soup" colors the water black.

Up until the discovery in 1977, scientists believed that life depended on sunlight. The first black smoker proved them wrong. Animals live deeper than sunlight reaches. The animals had never been seen before that discovery.

Near the vent, tube worms measure 7 feet (2 m) long and squeeze together. Their long, white shafts hide a feathery red fringe, more delicate than a rose. Basketball-sized clams and mussels as big as human feet cling to volcanic rocks. Pale pink, blue-eyed fish swim in water that smells like rotten eggs.

Scientists wondered how these creatures survive. The water could burn the flesh off a human being. The water pressure could crush a person

Deep-sea creatures glow in the dark. Check out this luminous viperfish. ▶

flat as a pancake. The mineral content in the water is poisonous to most living things. And there is no sunlight.

The answer to this puzzle is **bacteria.** The bacteria turn minerals and chemical compounds in the water into food and oxygen. Bacteria feed tube worms, clams, and other sea vent creatures. They allow animals to survive without the sun.

Since 1977, deep-sea dives have given scientists a new view of ocean life. Scientists have found hundreds of new animal species. New forms of life are discovered during nearly every dive. Only about 1 percent of the ocean floor has been thoroughly explored. No one knows what will be found in the remaining 99 percent.

? WORDS TO KNOW . . .

bacteria (back-TIHR-ee-uh) tiny living cells that can be seen only with the help of a microscope

9

The Human Touch

❧ A barge filled with garbage chugs out to sea. It goes several miles away from shore. Workers heave the cargo overboard. The trash is gone . . . or is it?

The garbage contained a mixture of paper, plastic, chemicals, metals, and rotting vegetable matter. The Styrofoam cups will take

500 years to decay. Plastic rings from six-packs of soda catch on seabirds and turtles. Soiled diapers and medical needles wash up on local beaches. Long after we die, that load of trash will still be affecting the ocean.

If a keystone species is one that changes an environment, then humans are keystone species of the oceans. No other species has created more change. No other predators have killed so many creatures. No other living beings have created quite as much mess in the oceans as humans.

Pollution

Pollution is caused by humans. The worst pollution comes from trash, chemicals, and oil spills. In the book *Sea Change*, Dr. Sylvia A. Earle reports, "Prior to 1988, the world's fleet of merchant vessels *every day* dumped at least 450,000 plastic, 4,800,000 metal, and 300,000 glass containers into the sea. . . . Until recently the United States Navy has typically thrown all wastes overboard. . . . A single large ship may generate more than 1,000 pounds [454 kg] of plastic trash a day!"

The government passes laws to prevent trash

READ IT!

Oceans for Every Kid by Janice Pratt VanCleave (John Wiley & Sons, 1996) offers dozens of science activities to do at the beach. No matter where your interests lie, VanCleave provides activities that are educational and fun.

◂ Barges loaded with garbage head out to sea to dump their cargo.

▲ Plastic bottles and other trash must be picked up to keep beaches clean.

🖐 **DO IT!**

Take part in the International Coastal Cleanup. This program, sponsored by the Ocean Conservancy, removes trash from beaches and wetlands. Recent efforts have collected more than 3 million pounds (1.4 million kg) of garbage from 6,887 miles (11,084 km) of coast. To find out about the next cleanup day, access *http://www. oceanconservancy.org.*

pollution of oceans and seas. However, no one can prevent people from littering beaches or tossing trash from boats. Some states and conservation groups sponsor coastal cleanups. These events yield thousands of pounds of plastic, paper, glass bottles, metal cans, cigarette butts, clothes, sunglasses, and even Barbie dolls.

Chemical pollution comes from factories and farms. A farmer in Indiana sprays his soil with liquid fertilizer. He douses his crops with pesticides to kill off insects. When it rains, chemicals are not absorbed into the ground.

Instead, they enter streams, then rivers, and finally our oceans and seas. A farmer who may have never seen the ocean just poisoned it.

The most dramatic pollution

! WOULD YOU BELIEVE?

There are "dead zones" in the seas where there is too little oxygen to support life. Dead zones can be found in the Gulf of Mexico and the Black Sea. Though some dead zones exist naturally, pollution contributes to the growth of these areas.

▲ Pesticides sprayed from this helicopter find their way to the ocean along streams and rivers.

South Africans reacted immediately when an oil spill threatened their coast in June 2000. The oil washed up on Robben Island, the home of 14,000 jackass penguins. Oil coated the penguins' feathers, which took away the feathers' waterproof nature.

The cleanup efforts on the island were demanding. Volunteers shoveled oily sand from the beach. Special cleansers were used to wash the rocks. Volunteers worked on their hands and knees, scrubbing away the oil.

Twelve thousand volunteers worked around-the-clock to save the birds. The penguins were airlifted by helicopter in cardboard boxes to a safe haven. Every penguin was washed thoroughly to remove the oil. After months of care, the jackass penguins received further medical checkups. Healthy penguins slipped into the ocean and headed home.

comes from oil spills. Huge tankers carry tons of oil across the ocean. When these tankers crash, sink, or leak, they spread oil on the seas. The oil covers the water and prevents sunlight from reaching marine plants. Oil slicks kill fish and seabirds by the thousands.

Marine mammals, such as seals and sea lions, depend on clean, dry fur to keep them warm. When coated with oil, fur loses its waterproofing. The animals also swallow the oil when they clean their fur. They get sick and die.

Too Much Fishing

Fishing creates its share of problems for ocean environments. This doesn't mean a weekend fishing trip with a

Fishing has gone high-tech since ▸ these men went to sea.

grandparent, but **commercial** fishing. Human beings have harvested food from the oceans for thousands of years. However, fishing changed as **technology** advanced.

Here is a comparison between fishing in 1910 and fishing today. In 1910, a ship loaded with fishers sets sail into the Gulf of Alaska. The ship hunts schooling fish. On the third day, they locate a school of pollock. The fishers work until the hold, or area of the ship that stores

▲ Today's catch will be cleaned, packaged, and displayed in the grocer's freezer in a matter of days.

cargo, is full. Then the fishers head back to port to deliver their fish.

Today, a fishing ship heads to sea with fishers and packers on board. The captain uses sonar to locate schools of pollock. As the fishers catch the pollock, the packers clean, cut, and package the fish.

Finished packages go into freezers. The ship's freezers can hold tons of frozen fish. The ship will stay at sea, catching fish almost daily, for three months.

The demand for fish in restaurants and supermarkets is great. Still, there comes a time when a species cannot

There's hardly room to anchor at this fishers' marina in Seattle, Washington. ▶

survive so much fishing. On North America's eastern coast, fishers struggle. They have overfished entire species, meaning there simply are no more fish to catch.

Humans have overfished cod, haddock, and shellfish. Great numbers of turtles have also been killed after being trapped and drowned in fishing nets. Marine mammals have not survived any better. Hunting whales, otters, seals,

and sea lions reduced many populations to near extinction. What is worse is that humans have not learned from their mistakes. Action to save endangered species does not come until a species can barely survive.

Whaling was an essential part of life for New Englanders in the 1700s and 1800s. Whale oil was used to light lamps before electricity. Whalebones supported umbrellas and a type of women's undergarment called a corset.

Gray whales no longer

live in the Atlantic Ocean. Other species, such as pilot, right, and bowhead whales, have dangerously low populations. There would be no right, pilot, or bowhead whales if the International Whaling Commission (IWC) had not been formed. Thirty-eight nations met in 1946 to discuss the worldwide situation for whales. They created the IWC.

The IWC had little success in stopping whaling until 1986. They decided then that people either had to stop hunting or there would be no whales left. Now, whaling is illegal. Only native people, such as the Inuit of Alaska, are allowed to hunt whales, although some countries still continue to hunt whales illegally.

People around the world still depend on fishing. Making fishing illegal is not

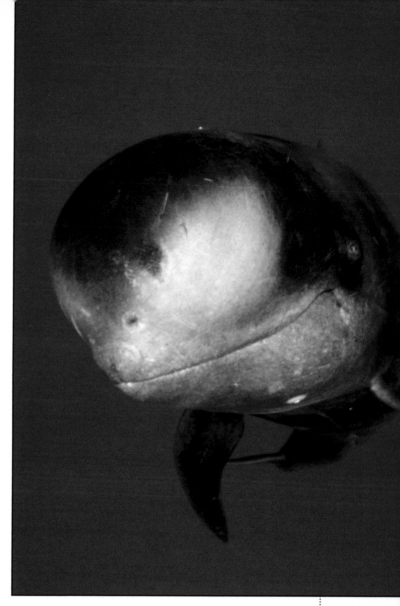

▲ As many as 50,000 pilot whales once swam the waters off Newfoundland, Canada. Whaling drove pilot whales nearly to extinction.

◄ New England seaports of the 1700s and 1800s depended on whaling to support their economy.

? **WORDS TO KNOW . . .**

aquaculture (AH-kwuh-CUHL-chur) farming fish and shellfish

possible. One solution to overfishing is **aquaculture.** Today, many fish and shellfish species are "farmed" fish. The fish are raised in beds. The number of fish harvested is managed so that the farm can continue to produce the fish. Common farmed fish include shrimp, crabs, oysters, catfish, tilapia, salmon, and trout.

Solutions for problems in our oceans and seas are not easy or simple. Governments pass laws to prevent oil spills and garbage disposal in the oceans. Other laws protect species, such as seals and sea lions, from hunting. International cooperation is necessary to enforce all these laws.

The government also sets up national and state

◄ A worker checks the size of salmon at a fish farm.

parks and preserves to safe-guard natural wonders. The Florida Keys, California's Channel Islands, and Texas's Flower Garden Banks are three marine sanctuaries protected by the government.

Private groups work to save the environment. Many of the groups deal only with ocean or sea life. The Ocean Conservancy and Greenpeace are two well-known agencies that defend ocean species.

The United Nations named several marine locations as World Heritage Sites. These are places of remarkable beauty and natural value. World Heritage Sites include the Great Barrier Reef and Shark Bay in Australia, Glacier Bay in Alaska, and the Belize Barrier Reef System in the Caribbean.

Education and

▲ California's Channel Islands are a sanctuary for sea lions and seals.

✋ **DO IT!**

Aquariums offer programs for kids and teens. Learn more about our oceans and seas. Take a class at an aquarium near you.

▲ Coastal Cleanup draws families who work to keep beaches clean.

effort are the keys to preserving ocean and sea ecosystems. People need to learn how to safeguard species and protect ocean life. Then, they must make the effort to put their knowledge into action. If not, dead zones will expand to include entire oceans. When the oceans die, so will almost all life on earth.

A rumble fills the air as the Muir Glacier calves in Glacier National Park, Alaska. ▶

Chart of Species

OCEANS AND SEAS	KEYSTONE SPECIES	FLAGSHIP SPECIES	UMBRELLA SPECIES	INDICATOR SPECIES
ARCTIC OCEAN	krill, plankton, sea otters	dolphins, whales, fur seals, walruses, polar bears	whales, walruses, polar bears	sperm whales, krill, plankton
ATLANTIC OCEAN	reef-building corals, krill, plankton, mangroves	dolphins, whales, loggerhead **turtles**	sea turtles, reef-building corals, gray whales, walruses	sperm whales, krill, plankton, reef-building corals, sea grasses
INDIAN OCEAN	reef-building corals, krill, plankton, mangroves	dolphins, Siberian cranes, **whales**	sea turtles, reef-building corals	sperm whales, sea grasses, plankton, krill
PACIFIC OCEAN	reef-building corals, krill, plankton, sea otters, kelp, mangroves	dolphins, Pacific gray whales, humpback whales, sea otters, fur seals	sea turtles, reef-building corals, walruses, sea otters, kelp	sperm whales, reef-building corals, kelp, dogfish sharks, krill
SOUTHERN OCEAN	krill, plankton,	dolphins, porpoises, orcas, minke whales, fin whales	southern fur seals, penguins, whales, albatrosses	whales, southern fur seals, krill
ARCTIC SEAS: BERING, CHUKCHI, BEAUFORT, LABRADOR	krill, plankton, shellfish	dolphins, orcas, humpback whales, gray whales	whales, walruses, polar bears, fur seals	whales, krill
TEMPERATE/TROPICAL SEAS: CARIBBEAN, MEDITERRANEAN, ARABIAN, GULF OF MEXICO	reef-building corals, krill, plankton, sea otters, mangroves, sea grasses	dolphins, manatees and dugongs, sea turtles, sea stars	sea turtles, reef-building corals, manatees and dugongs	reef-building corals, mussels, sea grasses, krill

▲ The above chart gives a starting point for identifying key species. Each ocean, sea, and reef environment has its own key species. The above chart lists some of those species.

[Bold-faced entries are the ones discussed in the text.]

[I n d e x]